Hidden in

When You Go Through Deep Waters

By

Sherna Williams

ROYSTON
Publishing

ISBN: 978-1-955063-82-1

Printed in the United States of America

Disclaimer: Photos included in this book are taken from actual hospital stays and post-surgical procedures.

over my family, you suited up and stood with me on the spiritual battlefield! This was "our" fight.

To my neighbor and friend, **Kelly Newland**: You "willingly" took on the responsibility of such an important need for us, and for that, we are eternally grateful!

To my neighbor and friend, **Lettie Tyson-Panwo**: Thank you for not only seeking God on our behalf but rallying the troops to pray with you!

I know this part is going to sound super weird but here's the deal. I am a transplant to Indiana, so my family resides far away. But my work family (**Brooke Lannan, Christy Davis, Whitney Arbuckle, Cheri Corley, Kelci Kidwell, Liz Nussbaum, Jamie Runyon-Heirs**) came all the way through! They LITERALLY stepped in and moved mountains for me when my world was falling apart.

To my twin, **Shanah Bannis**: When they see you, they see me and when they see me, they see you! Thank you for reading the manuscript and offering your spiritual insight.

To my family and friends from MILES away, who found a way to "touch" us despite the distance: **Sarah Robinson, Karla Tombrello, Novella Henry, Alex Sassaman, Kelly Newland, Tasia Eddy, Rayetta Anthony, Katie Dutt, Derick and Kylie Williams, Kristina Case, Emily Sowder, Amanda Deiterlin, Jennifer Wills, Christine Aaron, Stacie Krum, Omega Barro, Verna Baron**! You are my tribe!

When you go through deep waters, I will be with you.

When you go through rivers of difficulty, you will not drown.

When you walk through the fire of oppression, you will not

be burned up;

the flames will not consume you.

Isaiah 43:2 NLT

Table of Contents

Chapter 1
The Knowing

My 8-year-old daughter, Camille, created this art piece.
She sauntered around the house, gathering all the supplies
she would need, before finding a quiet place with the best
lighting. Nonetheless, if you looked closely beyond the
parts of the drawing that may appear seamless, you will
notice the erasures from her corrections. What you don't
see, though, are the moments of empty spaces and pause
within the journey of her creation. This is especially
important because it was within those moments she
allowed the true essence of herself to overflow, spilling
her strength, determination, and passion into the *details*
of this art piece.

...and so it was when God created you. He worked quietly
and carefully, as He poured himself within the *details* of
your story.

"For we are God's masterpiece.

He has created us anew in Christ Jesus, so we can do the

good things

He planned for us long ago."

Ephesians 2:10 NLT

Before you were formed in your mother's womb, the God of the universe single-handedly designed the masterpiece that is current your life…

Every twist and every turn

Every achievement and every set-back

Every high and every low

The bright days and the dark days

The moments of emphasis and the moments of pause

…represents the individual strokes of His hand because you are God's workmanship. Therefore, the *details* of your day-to-day are not random because He was very intentional with the creation of your story.

He not only planned the sequence of events in your life, but He also went ahead of you, to walk your very path so that He could strategically re-arrange the details of your

3

story *"for your good."* So while the situations you face in your day-to day may seem new, find courage in the *"knowing"* that Jesus stood exactly where you are standing right now, with you in mind.

Though I may not know your specific situation, my prayer for you is that you come to a place where you can, once and for all, break agreement with fear and worry because God is with you.

He has hidden himself within the *details* of your situation.

If you are anything like me, you would've raised your hand at this very moment, and asked, "Why is He hiding himself?" Then I would clasp my hands ever so gently, while stating, "Well, that is a great question, (insert your name here)!"

And you will seek Me and find Me,

when you search for Me with all your heart.

Jeremiah 29:13 NKJV

(Insert your name here), God hides Himself from those who have a casual heart toward Him, and instead reveals himself to those who diligently seek for Him through a prayerful relationship. He reveals Himself to those who search for Him as for hidden treasures (see *Proverbs 2).*

4

This is our story. I may not know your story, but I charge you to rest in *"the knowing"* that He is truly **Hidden in the Details**.

Chapter 2
Surprise from Heaven

My husband, Wayne, and I were content with our two girls. Life made sense. Adjusting our time, money, and resources was challenging but manageable for our two daughters. Between work, school, extracurricular activities, and planning family-time, we were thriving. Our day-to-day flowed beautifully within the natural rhythm of life. The girls were growing increasingly independent, which (uuhhhmm, yes, yes, yes) allowed for windows of quality time for my husband and me, both collectively and individually.

Needless to say, there wasn't anything or anyone in this world that could've convinced us another baby would be a great idea! We were in a groove *and* we had time on our hands (#goals).

So instead, God worked quietly and masterfully within the *details* of our lives to orchestrate His plan for our family because He wasn't quite finished with our story yet.

In October 2020, my husband and I were forced to address individual health-related circumstances.

My husband had lost his vision. He has an autoimmune disorder that primarily attacks his vision. So, if you can imagine all the challenges that could likely come with such a condition, you would understand why "grown-up time" was not on our radar at the time.

Then there was me: Sherna. I was diagnosed with endometriosis during the first year of my undergraduate studies. My symptoms were so severe at the time (2007) that I required surgical intervention.

In August/September 2020, I began experiencing an increase in related symptoms. By October 2020, I was desperate for relief and began considering a natural reset! After weighing my options, I chose to abstain from prescription medication for a short period of time, which (you probably guessed by now) included my birth control medication.

Yup, I can feel you picking up what I'm putting down, so go with it.

But, *in my defense*, I thought the timing of my "natural reset" was brilliant since Wayne and I were not in a position to entertain "grown-up time."

Well, clearly this entire situation with our health was a divine set-up because this happened in November 2020.

Chapter 3
Heaven on Earth

We gladly welcomed this surprise! We began planning and rearranging and were filled with excitement and anticipation! The girls were mind-blown at the thought of an actual baby in mommy's belly.

Safe to say, it was quite the fiasco when we found out the baby was a girl! We were all hoping for a boy (for "obvious" reasons...I mean, even the cat is a girl)! I laughed so hard that I probably cried. THREE girls, God? How did You figure this would be a great idea?

We named her Celeste, which means "Heavenly" and is quite fitting for this young lady, if I do say so myself.

But this pregnancy was different. It was so different that I considered attributing it to age (early 30s). However, things got dicey when I began experiencing health issues, and my bloodwork confirmed low iron levels. My iron levels were so low that I was plagued with heaviness while driving, would struggle to stay awake multiple times throughout the day, was severely nauseous and would become spontaneously shaky/jittery and uncontrollably emotional. Plainly put, I felt drunk all day.

I struggled to function and complete the most basic duties of my day.

We needed an intervention. Since I required sufficient blood levels in order to provide Celeste with a continual supply of blood to develop accordingly and avoid complications with her development and/or pre-term delivery, I began receiving iron transfusions during the third trimester of my pregnancy.

In addition to all of this, Celeste got comfortable very early on in my pregnancy. Once she found her sweet spot above my right hip bone, she remained there for the entire duration of my pregnancy. That was great for her and all, but as for me, her weight didn't distribute evenly as she grew in size. So, my right hip bore the entire burden of her development. This caused damage to my right leg. So, there were days where I was unable to walk for hours because the pressure was excruciatingly painful when I attempted to alternate legs while walking.

Since she remained in the lower right side of my body for several months, she pinched one of the nerves responsible for directing sensation to my right arm. As a result, I lost sensation in my right arm and fingertips. Between the damage to my right arm and right hip, I was left with a spinal cord injury.

Yet still, I prayed fervently for her health because sickness/disease is the not-so-distant cousin of death. It does not come from God and is the work of the Enemy.

So Satan went out from the presence of the Lord

and afflicted Job with painful sores from the soles of his

feet to the crown of his head.

Job 2:7 NIV

So, I submitted a prayer request at church because when the church prays, miracles, signs, and wonders break forth.

Again, I tell you that if two of you on earth agree about

anything you ask for,

it will be done for them by My Father in heaven.

For where two or three come together in My name,

there am I with them.

Matthew 18:19–20 NIV

After the Prayer Team submitted Celeste in prayer, God revealed information to one of the team members. God confirmed that Celeste would be born healthy, but her life would be surrounded by warfare because she is anointed and chosen.

I knew enough about spiritual warfare to know I needed to brace myself for life ahead.

The doctor recommended an induction at 39 weeks gestation.

Celeste Alanna Williams was born on Saturday, August 14, 2021.

Chapter 4
Divine Workmanship

I've always had a hard time imagining my babies, in actual human form, outside of my body. I find myself in such awe when I lay eyes on them for the first time, as if I had no clue I was pregnant, or there was a literal human growing inside of me.

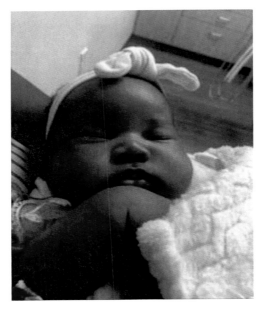

So, I was pleasantly surprised with this little number! She was gorgeous like her older sisters, at first glance! God did not hold back when He created her!

There is a something wonderfully unexplainable about her presence. She has a way of looking at you that will make you feel like you are the only one that matters in the world, and you are so specially loved by her.

I know what you're thinking—and no, I'm not just saying this because I'm her mom! This girl is truly something special. Don't take my word for it? Look for yourself!

Her sisters are smitten with her and so proud to call her their own! This little lady wants for nothing because her big sisters are always racing to the rescue! Watching the three sisters interact is a sight to see! The way her soul lights up in their presence takes my breath away each and every time.

All in all, life now makes sense in a way it never did before. I come alive when I hear the melody of their laughter in my ear.

See, even the cat is mesmerized by baby Celeste!

I ask her, each day, about the gift God hid in the depths of her being. I believe we are all called to a Kingdom purpose. But few of us are *chosen* to impact lives on a deeper level. God saw it fit to wrap her beautiful soul in flesh and send her to Earth to do something BIG for His Kingdom. I am honored to be her earthly mama!

Our family portrait is complete and boy, is it breathtaking!

Chapter 5
Life as I Knew It

Celeste and I attended her 4-month well visit. Once we were settled in the room and waiting for the pediatrician, I devoted all my efforts to keeping her warm and snug because she was required to remain in "only a diaper" until the pediatrician conducted her physical examination. So, I sat down in the chair and placed her in the sitting position with her back against my chest, making sure she was bundled tightly in her blanket.

When the pediatrician entered the room, he looked down into my lap to greet Celeste; however, his expression shifted quickly, as he squinted concerningly upon noticing the "odd shape" of the "top" of her head. He shared his concern that the top of her head was taking on a "bean-like" shape. He pressed gently against various parts of her head, as he measured the length and width of her head.

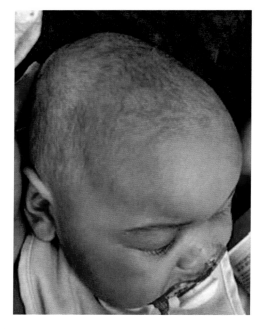

He explained, "It is likely the sutures on the left and right side of her head closed faster than the ones on the front and back of her head. As a result, her forehead is protruding out a bit and her head is taking on an elongated shape. If not corrected, her head will continue to balloon out rapidly in the front and back." He acknowledged, "There are specialists trained to assess these specific situations and make more conclusive determinations." We were referred to a "plastic surgeon" in the area.

If I'm being honest, the reality of the situation hadn't quite hit me at that point. I think the words "plastic surgeon" were the culprit because I, somehow, believed that this was not a big deal and would eventually blow over. I did not process the gravity of the situation. I think I even turned up the music in the car during my drive home from the pediatrician's office.

Three weeks later, I visited the plastic surgeon's office. I remember checking in at the front desk and chuckling to myself a bit because I never thought I would ever set foot in an *actual* plastic surgeon's office. The expansive waiting room boasted plush leather seating, with air-brushed professional photos/posters and pamphlets related to breast augmentation, smile lines, crow's feet and Botox®! MIRRORS were everywhere I turned! Everywhere!

Once we were checked in and settled in the room, we were told, "The doctor will be in shortly!" So, baby Celeste and I walked over to the full-length body mirror and proceeded to make faces and sing songs while we waited for the plastic surgeon. Once she got tired (okay, fine, it was me…"I" got tired), we sat down in the chair.

Shortly after, the plastic surgeon entered the room and introduced himself as the "cranio-facial surgeon."

That was when my world stood still.

He still hadn't quite looked at us yet. Upon entering the room, he walked over to the referral paperwork on the counter while asking, "What brings you in today?" When I began to recount my previous conversation with her pediatrician, he looked up at Celeste and announced, "Oh, I see it!"

He walked closer, bridging the gap between us so he could touch the skull of her head. Then, he measured her head. Celeste began fussing, so I instinctively caved my body inward over her little body while pulling away from the surgeon's touch.

I did not want him to touch her.

Not now.

Not ever.

Sensing the shift in my body language, he took a slow step backward. He gently explained, "Some babies are born with their skulls fully formed, in which case, they require a surgical intervention known as 'craniosynostosis.' Research has yet to identify the cause behind it. As of now, it appears to be a spontaneous event *in utero*. However, the opportunity for this intervention requires a specific age range in order to avoid any long-lasting impacts. If surgery is needed, we will cut into the top part of her head to remove the fusion (closure). If not, this could simply be a situation where she has to wear a helmet for some time, which is why we need to schedule a scan. If you feel right here (he touched the middle part of her head and gestured for me to do the same), I'm pretty sure this hard bone we feel is a sign that she does in fact have a fused skull. But let's schedule a scan so we are absolutely sure before making big decisions."

The cranio-facial surgeon explained, "If the scan confirms that she has a closed skull, we must move rapidly to schedule an emergency surgery."

Immediately, the air felt thick and heavy, as if I were moving against the current in a river's stream. Existing required so much energy that it felt unnatural. We barely made it to the parking garage before the tears began streaming violently down my face. Once Celeste was buckled safely in her car seat, I walked over to the driver's seat and cried uncontrollably. I had so many questions. I found myself thinking, "I am not strong enough for this situation. How could anyone be? This is my baby. ...cut into her head? How can any of this be real?"

Chapter 6
The Details

This was all taking place during a season of my life where I was STRETCHED. My husband lost his vision (again) approximately four months prior. So, I was EVERYTHING to my husband and three young girls.

But if it wasn't clear by now, I would like to go on the record as a Woman of God's Faith.

Naaah, not the "I read storybooks about Jesus" type…

No-no, not the "Devil is a scary, made-up monster" type…

Nope, not even the "I only go to church on Easter Sunday and Christmas Sunday," type.

You ready for it?

I am the "Jesus and I go way back to Sunday School, mid-week Bible study, Youth Night, Crusades, family devotion, youth retreats" type.

I am the "I am truly in awe of His omnipresence and providentially sovereign hands because we spend so much time together, and I experience so much of His favor in my life that I wonder how He's helping anybody else during the day" type.

I am the "Jesus is the first person I speak to when I open my eyes and before my feet hit the floor in the morning because I would not dare step into my day without His presence and His covering" type.

The Enemy truly hopes, with everything in him, that we believe he is a made-up figment of our imagination because when we take our eyes off the reality of who he is and live our lives in accordance with coincidence or happenstance, he advances.

You see, I didn't "happen" to have such severe bouts of anemia while pregnant that I almost fell asleep at the wheel (several times) while driving or almost delivered a pre-term, underdeveloped baby.

But the church prayed, and Celeste was a full-term, healthy baby because my favorite book (yes, you guessed it—the Bible) reminds us that the Enemy will come, but when we resist him, he flees *(see James 4:7)*.

…and no, that did not mean it was over. He simply went to do some more plotting because Celeste didn't "happen" to have a spontaneous skull closure, *in utero*, which has the potential to cause pressure on her growing brain, resulting in blindness, seizures, and intellectual and developmental disabilities.

But the church continued to pray, and there is not a doubt in my mind that God was working behind the scenes *before* we knew what was happening inside her beautiful little head.

Jesus reminds us that we will face trials in this life, but to take courage in Him because He's already overcome *ALL* of the attacks of the Enemy (see *John 16:33*).

So, while my mama heart was crippled with a pain so indescribable, I knew God was working because I serve the kind of God that comes down to meet me in the dark places of my life.

Priscilla Shirer said it best, in her sermon entitled "Identity in Christ". She explained that God meets us in the fire so we will "know what it feels like to have the presence of God cover us so comprehensively and so completely, that we will emerge from a season of life that felt like a furnace and not even have the smell of smoke on us."

So, as I continue to pen this journey, it will be my absolute pleasure to highlight the *details* for you.

Chapter 7
The Scan

Celeste's MRI scan was scheduled on my birthday, January 14, 2022, at 1:00 p.m. The medical team informed me that due to her age, she would require anesthesia/sedation during the scan and would need to fast for four to six hours before the scan. They also informed me that we would need to remain at the hospital for approximately two hours after the scan, in order for her medical team to monitor her bodily response to the anesthesia.

The week before the scan, Celeste presented with upper respiratory symptoms.

The day before her scheduled MRI scan, the hospital called to review procedures for the following day. When they learned about her symptoms, they shared that if Celeste presented with any symptoms the day of the scan, they would have to reschedule the procedure because her symptoms posed a concern for the anesthesia/sedation.

I heard everything the nurse explained, but she might as well have spoken to me in another language because as far as I was concerned, rescheduling was not an option given the time-sensitive nature of our situation. So, I began to thank God for what I already knew to be true— that she would not suffer from upper respiratory symptoms the next day and the scan would proceed as scheduled.

Celeste struggled with worsening symptoms throughout the entire night. But when we woke up the next morning, her symptoms had drastically subsided. I was relieved because I had a very specific plan to help her through the fasting period before her MRI scan. So, I immediately began feeding her servings of banana, oat cereal, and milk before her morning nap.

However, when I attempted to wake her at 8:30am for some additional fluids, Celeste vomited all (and I do mean "all") the contents of her stomach. Not only that, but she continued to repeatedly vomit. She became increasingly sad, lethargic, and lifeless as the vomiting turned into dry heaving. Each time she vomited, I felt an increasing sense of holy indignation.

My husband finally stated, "Babe, you should call the hospital and cancel the appointment because she is really sick. I just heard her stomach growl and if she does indeed fall asleep from all of this, we might as well feed her when she wakes. If you don't call and cancel this appointment, this will be an entire day wasted from work because they will likely send you back home."

I refused.

I responded, "No."

I refused to call and cancel the appointment because I had been praying too long and too hard to stand in God's way! As far as I was concerned, God was already involved.

When Celeste finally closed her eyes for another nap, I retreated upstairs to pack her bags, ready her car seat and lay her clothes out, because whatever the Enemy *thought* he was working on inside her beautiful head, the MRI scan would reveal and what the scan reveals is what I would pray against!

In the meantime, I prayed over her little belly, that God would fill her stomach with an overflow of HIS substance, that she would not get hungry during these next few hours before the scan and I thanked God for healing her body!

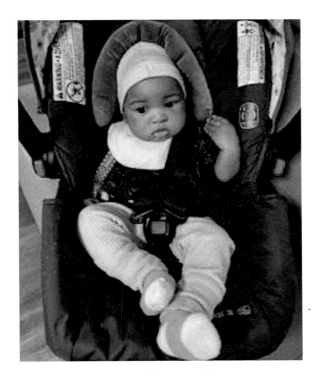

Hospital Waiting Room

Apparently, my God was working because when we arrived at the hospital, the excessive coughing of the past week, difficulty breathing, stuffiness, vomiting, fever, and lethargy from earlier that morning were all nonexistent. She never cried out of hunger! Not only that, but she was impressively alert!

She exuded a "Peace that transcends understanding" because even "I" didn't understand it after the morning AND WEEK we had!

We (and by "we," I mean party pooper over there) got tired while waiting for our turn in line.

Her medical team was so taken aback by her calmness (several nurses commented on her calmness), that they finally stated, "Mom, she is so calm that we have decided to do the scan without sedation. We will not do the anesthesia."

Such a weight was lifted from my mama-heart! Not only did we make it to through the visit without concerning symptoms but the part I dreaded the most for Celeste—sedation—was taken off the table!

Would you like to say it, or should I do us both a solid? Okay, I'll say it: **But God!!**

During the scan, she was so mesmerized by the colorful lights in the MRI machine, that she remained completely still. She did not cry or fuss. When the scan was over, we were free to leave the hospital within minutes.

Chapter 8
The Plan

I met with the neurosurgeon and the cranio-facial surgeon to discuss Celeste's scans. They presented a 3-D reconstruction of her brain. The "frontal view" of the scan confirmed that Celeste's sagittal suture was, indeed, closed off.

I didn't know I was holding in my breath until I tried to fight against a sudden burst of tears and almost buckled over. I'm unsure of what I expected to see or hear but the finality of the scan rocked my core.

I recorded the cranio-facial surgeon's explanation on a voice recording for my husband. He explained, "This is good because we caught it in time to get the best outcome that we need to treat this. When the sutures are closed, the skull does not expand in the direction of the closure. So, with Celeste, this is called a "sagittal synostosis," which means the growth center has fused in the midline. So, how do we treat this? We have to remove the piece of bone that is fused to allow the brain to expand in the rest of the skull. If we do nothing, the elongation can get worst and cause actual compression on the brain. So, we want to open it up so the brain can have room to grow. So, we remove the strip of bone. It's a pretty big surgery, but our goal is to allow the brain to breathe and grow. We don't know what caused this. So, it's nothing that you did or anybody did that led to this. There is nothing you could've done to prevent this. There may have been some genes involved, but most of the time it's just a spontaneous occurrence. We see quite a lot of these here, actually. We do a lot of them at this location and we have a whole team that's designated just for this, through our Cranio-facial Program."

The neurosurgeon explained, "I will make the incision at the top of her head and break the bone but there's a vein directly under the bone that runs the length of the bone, and that's the major risk because we absolutely cannot touch that vein for any reason whatsoever. So, we don't look at the clock. We are slow and careful. Our minds are clear and we can't be in a rush to get anywhere because nowhere matters but the surgery room. As a result, the surgery can take anywhere from seven to nine hours."

While looking at a scan of the 3-D imaging of her brain, the neurosurgeon shared, "Her brain is perfectly healthy and normal. There is no present impact, so we would rather move quickly with the surgery because if her brain continues to grow without this intervention, the closed skull can cause pressure on her growing brain. She will need to remain in the ICU for three to five days after the procedure."

So many words...

So much information...

It was as if I were standing at the edge of a cliff, with the weight of the wind beating violently against my face but…

I somehow needed to steady myself because one wrong move at the edge of this cliff and…

…down I go into the abyss.

Then I saw God *in the details.*

The neurosurgeon's voice echoed distinctly in my ears, as he explained, "Children with this condition typically have a prominent facial profile, but Celeste's forehead is smaller than what we typically see. She has such a mild physical presentation that it's a wonder the pediatrician even noticed this in the first place. What would've likely happened, is the pediatrician could've missed this and she would've grown up to be a regular girl. Then one day, seemingly unexpected, this would've come 'out of nowhere.'"

So, pardon me while I take this opportunity to tell you about the Divine Providence of God! God is always aware and therefore always working to strategically guide, steer and shift our situations and environments based on our needs. The world might call it *coincidence,* but it is because of **Divine Providence** that I <u>sat down in the chair</u> to bundle Celeste in her blanket, while waiting for her pediatrician. It was because of Divine Providence that I was *carefully positioned* in "just" the right way for her pediatrician to look down and *immediately see* what he needed to see because even when the Enemy bets against us, God controls the outcome.

Celeste was scheduled for surgery on Tuesday, February 8th, 2022. We were as prepared as humanly possible. We were fully informed, our bags were packed, and our close friends were ready to lend a hand whenever and wherever necessary during that time.

I read so many beautiful, heartfelt messages and prayers from family, friends, and even strangers near and far. I am so grateful for each person that lifted our girl in prayer to Heaven that day. While I waited for this nightmare to be over, I gave myself permission to be still beneath the covering of those prayers.

Chapter 9
Kingdom Peace

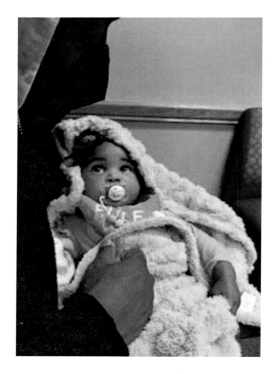

Surgery Day

During Monday Morning Prayer, Pastor Rooks instructed us on fully embracing *God's Peace*. He explained that God originated and is the founder of *Peace*. *Peace*, in the world, is contingent on feelings, and is therefore inconsistent, changes with our situations/circumstances, and creates desperation.

However, *Kingdom Peace* is a fixed reassurance based on God's view of the situation.

When Pastor Rooks prayed with us on the morning of the surgery, he prayed for *God's Peace*.

He confessed *God's Peace* over our hearts and minds, and especially over Celeste (see *Philippians 4:7*).

He confessed *God's Peace* over us because, according to God's view, the surgery was already successful and she was already healed (see *Isaiah 53:5*).

He confessed *God's Peace* because, according to God's view, she will satisfy Him with long life (see *Psalms 91:16*).

He confessed *God's Peace* because, according to God's view, the victory over her health had already been won (see *Corinthians 10:13*).

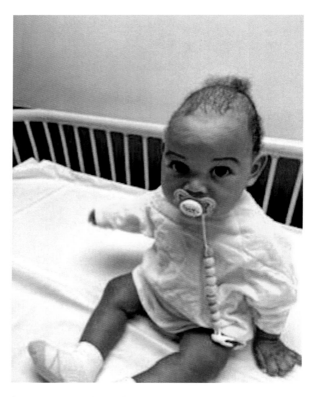

After the nurse took Celeste's vitals, she instructed me to change Celeste into the hospital gown provided. My fingers shook violently, as I placed the gown over her body. *"Peace," I reminded myself.*

The gown was a soft, beautiful canary yellow. I reminded myself, "This is your favorite color. Remember what you explain to everyone when they ask about your favorite color? You tell them that you love yellow because it's bright and contagious. You tell them that simply looking at the vibrancy of the color brightens your mood." So, I willed myself to look at the color and I mean, *really* look at it because…there He was again, *hidden in another detail*. "*Peace,*" *I reminded myself.*

I took the most precious time, as I tied the neck strings and waist strings of the gown into perfect little bows on her back, as if it was the least I could do and it counted for something.

But the tears escaped and trickled down my cheeks like water quickly running off into the stream on a rainy day. "*Peace,*" *I reminded myself.*

I gave her kisses, held her close and whispered, "I love you. I will be waiting right here for you." I reminded her (and myself) that we "already prayed and served notice to Heaven. So, the angels will be waiting to greet you in the operating room." "*Peace,*" *I reminded myself.*

Eventually, the nurses arrived to transport her to the surgical suite. They explained they would call me right after the first incision and every hour after that with updates. One nurse explained, "It takes a little over an hour to do the anesthesia, blood banking (in the event a transfusion is necessary), positioning, catheter and IV placement. So, do not be alarmed if you don't receive a phone call right away."

Then the other nurse said, "Mom, I'm going to hold her in my arms instead of wheeling her away in the crib. It's easier that way."

"Peace"… "PEACE," I tried to remind myself.

My soul finally cried out to God, "I cannot do this! I've changed my mind about all of it! I can't **MAKE** my body do it! I can't **GIVE** her to them. I can't **LET** them cut her head open. There has to be another way!"

…then His soft, still voice responded.

He said, "Place her in **My** arms. Give her to **'Me'** instead. Keep the eyes of your heart fixed on **'Me.'** Do not look at them. Give her to **'Me.'"**

I closed my eyes and inhaled sharply. *"Peace," I reminded myself.*

I handed my beautiful, perfect girl over at approximately 8:03 a.m. and quickly turned around to face the wall, so I could force myself to remain in position. *"Peace," I reminded myself.*

...because every part of my being yearned to follow them, take her back from them or, at minimum, watch her as she disappeared with them down the long hallway.

I cried for two whole hours. Yes, I depended on God for *Peace* over the surgical procedure and knew, without a doubt, that the surgery would be successful but my heart was broken.

I received the first phone call at 10:04 a.m., informing me that the neurosurgeon had "just made the first incision." *"Peace," I reminded myself.*

At 11:40 a.m., I received the second phone call, informing me, "Celeste is stable. The neurosurgeon has completed his procedure and the cranio-facial surgeon is prepping to enter the operating room to do the closure." *"Peace," I reminded myself.*

Shortly after, the neurosurgeon entered the waiting area to brief us. He held his hand to his heart and expressed, "These surgeries can get really hairy because we can't touch certain veins and we have to be really careful but I'm so grateful because she gave me such a *peaceful experience. It was so peaceful.* My part was a cakewalk. Everything went so smoothly. I do quite a bit of these and *it's usually not this easy! So that made me feel so good inside!"*

"Peaceful."...because when God is in the room, He serves notice to EVERY HEART.

At 12:20 p.m., the cranio-facial surgeon walked into the waiting room. He shared, "Everything went as planned. Her head is already beginning to expand. She lost very little blood, so no transfusion needed. We didn't have to implement any emergency protocols. Everything was easy and smooth."

"Easy and Smooth."...because God was *in the details* again, a seven- to nine-hour surgical procedure was accomplished in less than four hours, and He did not leave the surgeons' hearts untouched!

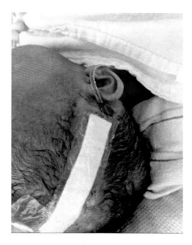

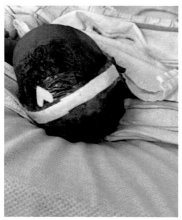

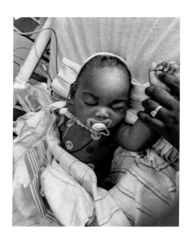

After being released from Recovery, Celeste was transported to the Pediatric Intensive Care Unit. When we first laid eyes on her, we were at a loss for words because she was connected to several different wires. She was still under the effects of the anesthesia, so her eyes were closed but she was moaning and crying out in pain. She required morphine every three hours. When she "came out of it," she drank fluids with a vengeance. With each passing hour, she gained more control.

Peace.

Chapter 10
Permission Granted

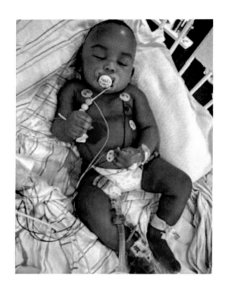

Pediatric Intensive Care Unit

If you asked me weeks prior (even days), to imagine a
world where I was not allowed to hold her for over
twenty-four hours or a world where she was suffering
something unimaginable right before my very eyes, but
all I could do was stand and bear witness, I strongly
believe my mind would've glitched.

Celeste developed a surgical fever that spiked
continuously throughout the day. I held her little hands as
she cried through uncomfortable rectal temperature
checks, the burning in her little arms when they flushed
her IV multiple times a day, the spikes of pain and

pressure when her medication wore off, her body writhing in pain from the insertion of rectal suppositories, blood draining through the tube connected to the opening in her skull, discomfort from the catheter in her diaper, ongoing soreness in her throat from the breathing tube, pain and discomfort from resulting facial swelling, and the physical weariness from it all.

Somewhere along the way, I lost the ability to distinguish her cries of pain from her cries of frustration, especially after we were cautioned against side-sleeping and directed to keep "the Professional Side-Sleeper (this is literally her full-time job)" positioned on her back at all times, in order to help the back of her head round out accordingly. My sweet baby was unhappy and struggling to make it from one hour to the next without my embrace.

The following day, we paused to celebrate and breathe a
little when we received news that she was no longer
considered "critical." I held her little hands tight and my
heart beamed with relief as they removed most of the

"many cords and wires" connected to her little body. I was finally able to hold her close! The depth of that moment, chest-to-chest heart-to-heart, was indescribable. Shortly after, we were released from the PICU to a hospital room on the general floor.

But later that day, Celeste woke up from an afternoon nap with her eyes swollen shut. She cried out inconsolably, as she flailed around with outstretched hands in search of me. She was afraid and alone in the darkness of her own being, and I could not fix it. I cried softly, as I tried to hold her little hands but that did not seem to help. The swelling also caused blood to pool and escape around the tube connected to the opening in her skull. So, I watched as more and more blood escaped the tubing, building enough momentum to create a puddle big enough to drip slowly down her neck, and roll purposefully down her chest. I could barely make out the muffled voices of her Care Team, but every now and then, my mind registered the words "normal" and "expected" and "lasting weeks-to-months."

So, I sang one of our favorite songs.

Jesus loves Lessie, this I know.

For the Bible tells me so.

Little Lessie to Him belongs.

Lessie is weak, but He is strong.

…she immediately hushed and whimpered quietly as she leaned into my shoulders.

I continued to sing.

Yes, Jesus loves Lessie.

Yes, Jesus Loves Lessie.

Yes, Jesus Loves Lessie.

The Bible tells me so.

I sang, over and over, as she listened closely with her heart. I listened with my heart too, especially when I sang *"Lessie is weak, but He is strong."*

…because it seemed we both needed a reminder that He continues to exist *in the details* of our weak moments. We needed a reminder that an expectation of strength was never required for this journey but rather, permission is always granted to be weak in the *knowing* that He is strong. Once we knew what we were looking for, it was easy to see the provision of His strength tightly woven *in the details* of that moment. So, we leaned into it for the night.

Chapter 11

Hidden in the Details

The next day, Celeste's Care Team assured me that her facial swelling was "normal." They shared, "We see it all the time with these cases. That's how these surgeries go. I've discharged babies home and they've either looked like this or worse but it should go back down. It will resolve itself within a few days, weeks or possibly even months."

The nonchalance in their responses puzzled me because as far as I was concerned, **MY BABY'S EYES WERE SWOLLEN SHUT**, she couldn't see and was scared. I felt myself getting angry, as my face flushed, my heart pounded faster, and my tone darkened a bit.

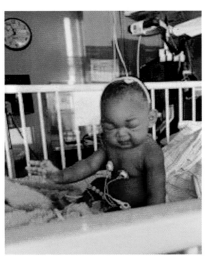

So, I paused and turned to look at Celeste closely. In that moment, I immediately felt her lostness in a world where she should exist but somehow couldn't. I observed her disappointment when she turned her head to a sound or a light, in hopeful anticipation of some "thing" or some "one" to look at, but…nothing. I noticed how she breathed deeply in relief, whenever I laced my fingers into hers, as if my touch was food to her soul. I felt the fierceness in her little grip, as if she were beckoning me to "never let go!"

It was in that moment that I realized I was letting my spiritual guard down.

Yes, the surgery was successful, but the Enemy never said it was over! He still had an assignment to complete: *Prevent her, by any means necessary, from reaching the destiny God had assigned to her.*

So, it remains his job to watch her closely, in search of an unsuspecting opportunity for pursuit.

That moment—her long-term health—was the unsuspecting opportunity for pursuit. Therefore, he was counting on me listening solely to the doctors or pointing my fingers in anger because as long as my eyes were trained on the doctors, I would let my guard down and take my eyes off of him.

But the Word of God is clear:

We battle NOT against flesh and blood

Ephesians 6:12

I absolutely understood what the *research* reported and how it turned out for *other people*, but I had a **DIVINE** expectation for this story to end differently.

So, I took *Authority* **in the** *Name of Jesus* and stood in the gap for my daughter. I held my stance of faith in prayer, confessed abundant life over her, and cancelled all the schemes of the Enemy. I told Pastor Rooks, "I heard what the doctors had to say about why she was so swollen and unable to see but the **BLOOD OF JESUS** speaks a better word over **ALL** words."

As the day went on, the nurses began commenting, "Oh my, her eyes are opening back up!" or "I heard the other nurse mention that her swelling is already going down, so I had to see it!" or "Did you see her right eye is opening at the bottom?"

Just in case you're still missing it, My God was actively working on our behalf and was making it known by leaving *the details* behind for all to see.

Later that afternoon, one of the other doctors came by to remove the bandage from her wound and the drain tube connected to the opening in her head. He shared, "The purpose of the tube is to allow an escape for the blood and avoid blood clots from the pooling of blood inside her head. But the blood coming out through the drain has decreased significantly over the last few days. Therefore, it is time to take it out and remove the bandage over her wound."

To say this was a painful process for Celeste would be such an understatement! The doctors even permitted me to leave the room because. . .well, they knew.

While I held her hands, rubbed her back, and prayed to God for her strength, my best friend stood with me, as she held my hand, rubbed my back, and prayed to God for my strength. As the doctor ripped the sticky tape away from the incision on her head with all his might and as fast as he could, Celeste locked eyes with me, as she *scream-cried* something fierce and never ever looked away from me. Surrendering all my strength to her, I did not break eye contact with her as he pulled and tugged and pushed against the raw, fresh wound on her little head. Her soul-cringing cries ricocheted around my head, as if her entire being was aflame. In the end, her face and neck were drenched in sweat and tears.

But, to my surprise, the doctor did not stop there. He quickly transitioned to removing the drain tube connected to the incision in her head. As he pulled and pulled, her tiny body writhed in pain. She tried to escape his hands, as she attempted to slide from her sitting position and unto her back. As heart-wrenching as it was, I held her in place while looking deep into her soul because...well, she didn't know this, but I knew that if I allowed her to slide away, it would prolong this process for her. So instead, I endured with her.

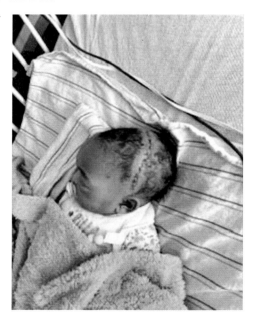

Later that evening, the neurosurgeon stopped by and announced, "I'm here to see the Angel baby!" He still remembered the *"Peace"* he felt in the operating room during her surgery that Tuesday morning.

"...the angels will be waiting to greet you in the operating room."

...and so it was, because when her loved ones and even strangers from near and far called down Heaven on her behalf, Angels responded and flooded her operating room.

The next morning, this happened.

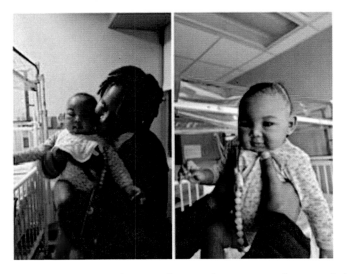

The swelling in her face and eyes disappeared over night.

A few hours later, we were discharged **without** pain medication. The discharging doctor stated, "I was reviewing her chart and saw that she hasn't required any heavy pain medication since Wednesday morning and even the Tylenol is now every six hours instead of every three hours. That's impressive after such a major surgery because this was a pretty big operation. Usually, we have to send off prescriptions to the pharmacy, but you guys are good to go!"

…and there He was again, *in the details* of it all.

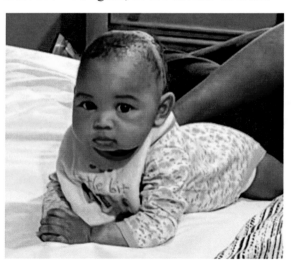

Home, Sweet home (few hours after discharge)

May 2022 – Baby Dedication

May 2022 – Baby Dedication

Dear Reader,

I wish I could sit across from you, so you can openly share your fears and trials, too. My soul yearns to hold this burden with you and create space for your pain because God knows I can relate. But instead, allow me this opportunity to pen a message to your heart.

The God of Heaven goes before you, to carefully sift through the events of your life. Therefore, if He allowed your current circumstance to come to pass, He intended to use it for your good. Your current circumstance is an assignment from the Enemy to destroy your mind by tarnishing your hope. Your world is closing in from all sides, and it feels as if there is no way out. But I want to remind you of a major technicality in your favor. God provided a means of escape for you when He declared:

And we know
that all things work together for good
to them that love God,
to them who are the called according to His purpose.
Romans 8:28 KJV

But He does require one thing from you: **your focus**. In this life, we will face hardships, but your pain can have purpose if you fix your eyes on Him.

You see, where your focus goes, your faith flows, and you are so focused on your circumstance that you are unknowingly magnifying the gravity of the situation and missing out on the best part: **Him**.

Although I am hopeful that you were indeed able to experience God through my journey, I so wish I could take you back to a few other moments.

I wish you saw the many times fear and doubt crept in.
I wish you saw how trying it was to maintain my faith stance when I was being stifled with weariness and weighted with fatigue.
I didn't tell you about the sacrifice, obedience, and submission required to "stand in the gap," for my infant daughter during the long nights and lonely days.
I wish you saw how physically tired I truly was.

But today, my daughter is healthy and whole because I fulfilled the requirement to fix my eyes on Him. I commanded my soul to trust Him when I didn't understand, didn't see Him and didn't feel Him.

Jesus said, "Blessed is he who have not seen but still believe" (see *John 20:29*).

So, let the phrase "in all things" be the daily meditation of your soul.

Even in this thing…your thing.
Trust Him all the same.

If you reconciled your spirit with this request, you will experience a sense of *"knowing."* The deep desperation, unsteadiness and daunting feeling that existed in the pit of your stomach should be greatly minimized because when you lean into the Spirit of God within you, you receive access to divine truth.

God is with you and when God shines His face upon you, His Spirit within you *"knows"* before you do, how your story will unfold. This *"knowing"* will yield *Divine Peace*. Follow the lead of the Holy Spirit and lean into the *"knowing,"* allowing yourself to come into agreement with the *"peace that surpasses all understanding"* (see *Philippians 4:6–7*) because God is sovereign and has the power to overturn and reverse ALL things.

The truth is God is always with you, **Hidden in the Details.**

May, 2022 – Baby Dedication

Chapter 12
Hesed Movement

"God will sustain those who belong to Him in unstable seasons." Those were the words of comfort God imparted to me, through Pastor Julien Rooks, of Christian Muscle Wellness Academy.

When I recount this experience, for those who were not aware, I always say, "It felt like I was properly positioned in every way."

You see, before God allowed my family to journey through this experience, He had already provided the tools and created the environment for us to thrive through it.

He wasn't only **Hidden in the Details** of Celeste's surgery and healing but He was also **Hidden in the Details** in such an unexpectedly personal way. His light shown through friends and family, as He extended Godly favor to us, reminding us that He is, in fact, Jehovah Jireh (our provider).

To name a few, friends and family provided onesies, blankets and teddy bears for Celeste's hospital stay and inspirational reminders, motivational messages, and audio books to support my mental/emotional well-being. God even took it up a notch and facilitated three meals each day at the hospital and a meal train during our first week home from the hospital.

But mostly, I was in awe of His Grace and how He loved me so intentionally. There is only one way to describe a loving-kindness so undeserving, so personal, and that goes beyond the requirements of duty: *Hesed*.

Hesed is not a feeling but an action that symbolizes all the positive attributes of God. Author Lois Tverberg explained that *Hesed* "intervenes on behalf of loved ones and comes to their rescue."

"Hesed Movement" is a Christian-based re-distribution non-profit that seeks to extend God's love to families needing support during difficult journeys of medical challenges. We collect unsold toys, clothes, blankets, and bibles, as well as provide meal cards, snacks, and grocery cards, in the form of care packages, to the parents of infants/toddlers in hospital-based settings. Care packages will include (but are not limited to): Bible, autographed copy of *Hidden in the Details*, meal/grocery card, personal item for baby/toddler, personal item for parent, customized T-shirt.

At **Hesed Movement**, we're not just another care package delivery service. We are passionate about putting God's love, faithfulness, mercy, grace, kindness, and loyalty "into action" by being the hands and feet of Jesus.

When you partner with **Hesed Movement**, you not only say "yes" to introducing others to the perfect and enduring love of God but you help lighten the load, on such a personal level, for families in hospital settings near and far, regardless of background or affiliation.

When you donate to our cause, you will receive a Prayer Wall email alert each time **Hesed Movement** provides a care package to a family. We aim to surround families with our community of believers.

For more information and updates, email us at: hesedmovement@gmail.com.

Dedication

For my girls:

Camille (my twinkle *Star*)

Jolie (my only *Sunshine*)

Celeste (my little *Light*)

Acknowledgment

First and foremost, I would like to give praises to **My God** because this book would not exist without His divine wisdom and guidance. I am honored to bring glory to His Name because the "joy of the Lord is my source of strength."

To my husband, **Wayne Williams**, for believing in me so much that he willingly partnered with me on this journey, celebrated my highs, and dusted me off during my lows.

To my family who always "saw me," even when I didn't see myself: **Joseph and Athinia Bannis; Yvonne Williams; Trevy, Benjamin**, and **Benilia Bannis; and Melisa Rivera-Bannis.**

To my best friend, **Sheryl-Ann Suffren**: You gave me rest when life tossed me to and fro!

To my sister from another mister, **Keshia Porter**: Thank you for wearing ALL my hats! You were willing to be whatever version of me that my daughters needed, whenever they needed it.

To my spiritual sister, **Tiffany Grahn**: So many people believed I was capable of being an author, but you made it your DAILY mission to hold me accountable to writing this book, cheered me on every single step of the way, read drafts (excitedly) and made me feel like a famous author before I believed this was possible for me.

To my Pastor, **Julian Rooks**, and my **Christian Muscle Wellness Academy** family: When the Enemy declared war